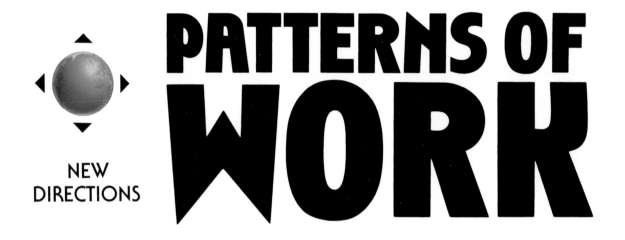

NEW
DIRECTIONS

PATTERNS OF WORK

Judith Condon

Franklin Watts

New York   London   Toronto   Sydney

CONTENTS

©1992 Franklin Watts

Franklin Watts
95 Madison Avenue
New York, NY 10016

Series devised by
Rosalind Kerven

Editor
Ruth Taylor

Picture researcher
Sarah Moule

Designed by
Geoff Francis

Library of Congress Cataloging-in-Publication Data

Condon, Judith.
    Patterns of work/by Judith Condon.
    p. cm. – (New directions)
    Includes index.
    Summary: Examines new trends in the work force due to unemployment, new technology, changing roles in family life, and increased longevity.
    ISBN 0-531-14228-0
    1. Labor market–Juvenile literature.
2. Unemployment–Juvenile literature. 3. Technological innovations–Juvenile literature. 4. Family–Juvenile literature. 5. Longevity–Juvenile literature.[1. Work. 2. Labor.] I. Title. II. Series: New directions (New York, N.Y.)
HD5706.C626 1993   92-7838
331.1–dc20   CIP AC

Printed in Belgium

How Work Developed

From the earliest times people worked to provide themselves with food, warmth, and shelter. Their patterns of work helped shape both their understanding of the world and the societies they built. At first they lived in small communities, hunting and gathering food, collecting fuel, and keeping safe from wild animals or enemies. As agriculture developed, and tools were improved, work grew more specialized. Some people became skilled at pottery, some at weaving cloth. They exchanged goods by barter, and eventually they devised the money system.

A new class of workers dealt with measuring, weighing, and keeping records. Others passed on history and culture, including religion. Their knowledge and skills, their books and mathematical tables were highly prized and closely guarded.

Over the centuries forests were cleared, new crops developed, and the population grew. Most people worked on the land. Other skilled trades were carried on mainly in the towns. Frequently the whole family took part in the work. But women were not allowed to achieve the status of "master craftsman," and boys had to serve long apprenticeships. Some craftsmen formed guilds and became powerful in the local community. In most Christian countries hard work was thought to be godly, and idleness to come from the devil. Only the very rich were allowed time for leisure.

Increasingly traders traveled to faraway places. In the late fifteenth century, European adventurers reached the American continent and began to found colonies. By force of arms they imposed their culture, including their ideas about work, on the local populations. They also cruelly transported Africans across the ocean to work as slaves on their sugar and cotton plantations.

Patterns of work shape city life. This traffic jam is in Karachi, Pakistan, but the same rush-hour congestion occurs in industrial cities all around the world.

The Industrial Revolution

In the eighteenth century, in Britain, the invention of steam-powered machinery transformed the world of work. Large wool and cotton mills took over from home-based hand-loom weavers and spinners. Poverty drove people from the countryside into fast-growing industrial towns. Factory owners who had invested money in machines wanted to get as much out of them as possible. Production was broken down into small repetitive tasks; children and adults worked long hours for low pay, and had to live and work in appalling conditions.

Charles Chaplin's famous film Modern Times *depicts a worker caught in the power of vast machines. The film was a satire on what it felt like to work in an American factory in the 1930s.*

As industrialization spread to other countries, the same patterns developed. Cities and towns spread outward, with large factories - often belching out pollution - on one side, and housing on another. A busy network of public transportation grew, getting people to work and home again. As industry and society became more complex, workers needed to be able to read and write and do basic arithmetic. Mass education was introduced. Now many people made their living as teachers and clerks. Meanwhile, working-class people organized for and won the right to vote, and began to gain better pay and conditions.

In the United States, **mass production** reached a new pitch when Henry Ford introduced into his Detroit car plant a conveyer belt moving **production line**. People had to work at a constant speed - or else be fired. As other employers followed suit, each task was "scientifically" measured and speeded up for maximum efficiency. Workers earned better wages, but they suffered the effects of noise, stress, and boredom.

New Technology

Since the 1960s new technology has brought another revolution to the world of work. Ever more powerful computers can make rapid calculations, and store and manipulate huge quantities of information. In Japan, the United States, and Europe few workplaces now operate without them. Other innovations, such as television, communication by satellite and fiber optics, allow messages to be relayed instantaneously around the world. More and more people work in the information industry - in journalism, in business research, or conducting surveys of public opinion.

In recent years certain jobs have disappeared, and many people - sometimes whole communities - have been thrown out of work. For example, intensive farming uses sophisticated machines and chemicals to replace the farm laborer, while in some factories robots have taken over tasks such as fixing components or spraying paint. Employers feel that without this technology their products will not be as good or as cheap as those of their competitors. But the human cost, measured in unemployment, has been high. Some people have been drawn into the expanding "service sector" - working in stores, banks, and jobs to do with leisure, while others have been given training for the increasing number of jobs based mainly on "brain" skills.

The megachip seems to hold endless potential for changing our working lives.

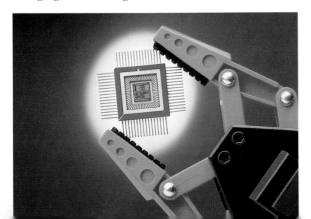

In some parts of the world people subsist on small areas of land. In Zambia, as in many parts of Africa, most food is grown by women working long hours with very basic tools. In Malawi, East Africa, 90 out of every 100 workers still work on the land, whereas in the United States only 3 out of 100 do so.

Workers' Rights and Human Rights

While heavy manual labor has declined in richer countries, many of the more unpleasant jobs have simply shifted elsewhere. In some parts of the world workers are exploited as badly as those in Britain two hundred years ago.

In some countries, working life has been hugely improved. **Trade unions** are able to speak up for their members, to gain better pay and conditions. In the 1980s the Polish trade union Solidarity even helped topple that country's repressive government. In other places progress is held back - sometimes by restrictions on human rights. In Saudi Arabia, the United Arab Emirates, and Sudan, trade unions are banned. In Egypt workers are forbidden to go on strike, and in South Korea and Iraq their leaders have been thrown into prison and even executed.

This book is about some new approaches to the many issues that affect working life. It describes steps to rethink and remake the changing world of work.

Since the end of the 1960s, not only new technology but also new ideas have affected our patterns of work. In the United States, the civil rights movement, closely followed by the women's liberation movement, challenged established patterns and prejudices. Why, they asked, were jobs traditionally done by black people and women given low pay and low status? Why, even when people did equal work, did they not receive equal rewards?

The women's movement also raised questions about work within the home. Why shouldn't men and women share both the hard work and the satisfaction of raising their children? Why should a man expect a woman to do all the housework and cooking? Why should men be judged solely in terms of how much money they earned?

These themes were quickly taken up in Britain and other European countries. Over the last twenty years they have profoundly affected the way employers, governments, and individual men and women think and act.

New ideas also came from the new environmental movement. Here, too, people asked questions beginning with "Why?" Why is western society so geared up to producing more and more goods, many of which are harmful to the planet? Why do we all work so hard to maintain a life-style – eating over-rich food, smoking, drinking too much alcohol, rushing from place to place – which is positively harmful to us? Are we to blame for spreading this way of life to people in developing countries? "Green" thinkers argued that we would be better living in a simpler, less wasteful way, allowing ourselves time to play as well as work. Perhaps we have something to learn from non-industrial societies, where people's work is more in tune with the natural environment.

As a result of all these questions, focus has turned in a more philosophical way toward the needs of the individual person. To be fulfilled, each of us needs work, paid and unpaid, that is satisfying and useful. It should be work of which we can be proud: not done against our principles, or just for pay. What is more, in the course of our lives we can expect to do many kinds of work, carrying with us skills that are useful in personal as well as working life. In fact, our aim should be to overcome the false separation between life and work, and become more whole again.

This nurse has the personal satisfaction of knowing that her work is appreciated by others, and that it fulfills a worthwhile purpose.

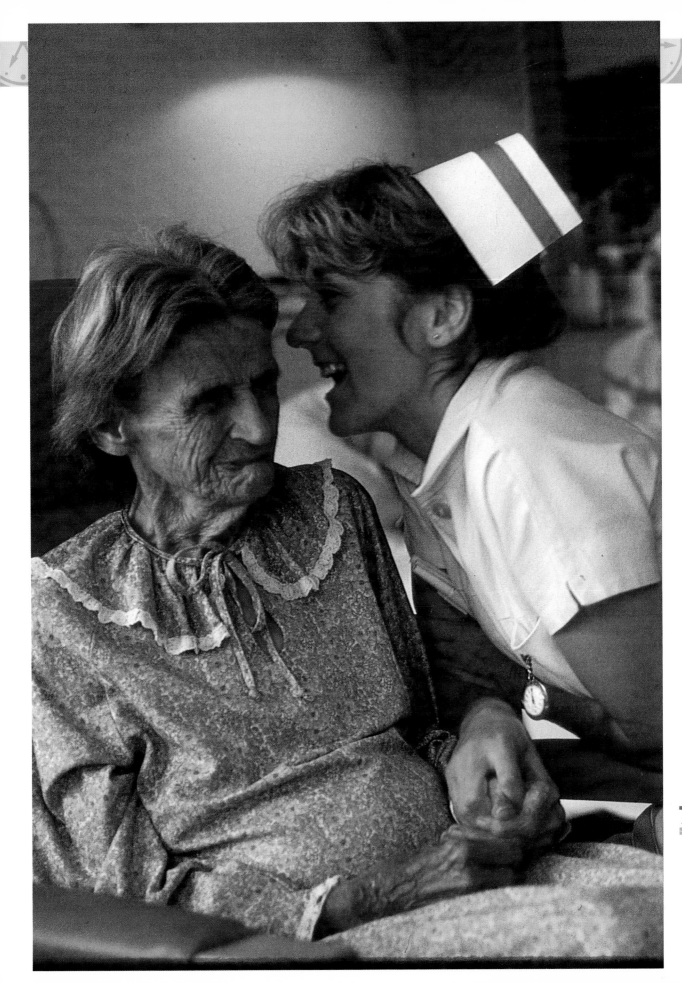

COGS IN A MACHINE

Ironically, this ugly office complex houses the British government's Environment Department. Like many "sick buildings" of similar design, it is soon to be demolished.

Every morning, in cities around the world, millions of people spill out of trains, buses, and cars on their way to work; every evening they travel back to the suburbs – a vast army of workers on the move. Each year many go further afield, perhaps working thousands of miles away under contract, or migrating permanently to another region or country in pursuit of work. The distances people travel are a sign of how, in industrial societies, "work" and "home" have become separated.

The typical workplace has also become larger and more anonymous. Industrial processes are concentrated in ugly buildings on industrial estates; administration, banking, and insurance are located in high-rise office complexes, crowded into the city center. All too often human health, safety, and comfort are low down the list of priorities when

workplaces are designed. Workers worldwide suffer lung damage from breathing in coal dust or asbestos; injury from avoidable accidents; or poisoning by dangerous chemicals – any of which can result in death. Some modern offices have been called "sick buildings" because the air-conditioned atmosphere and artificial lighting cause people to become ill. Many workers suffer stress, or back pain, or repetitive strain injury – a painful condition first found in the hands of chicken pluckers, but now common among typists and computer operators. Research in Britain and Sweden shows that a third of all ill-health and disease can be linked directly or indirectly to people's work.

Bringing Work to People

Busy cities such as New York and Los Angeles are so unpleasantly congested that employers may find it hard to

recruit skilled people to come to work in them. Several American companies have moved into the suburbs in order to recruit office workers, especially women. One extreme example is the case of the New York Life Insurance Company, which opened a claims office in Ireland. Here it found a well-educated work force in a region glad

to have new jobs. Modern telecommunications make for easy contact with the home office back in New York.

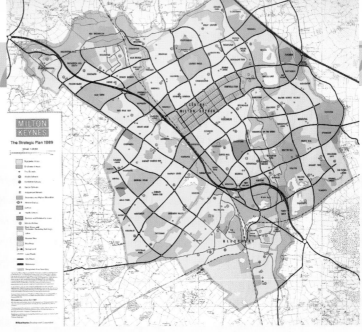

A City to Live and Work In

In 1967, 22,000 acres of Buckinghamshire, England, were set aside for a new city called Milton Keynes. The development master plan provided for a wide variety of jobs and houses, with commercial and industrial sites distributed through the city instead of being concentrated in one part. Factory buildings are landscaped so as not to spoil the attractiveness of residential areas. Linear parks create ribbons of green space, and there are plenty of pedestrian and bicycle routes.

Plan of the city of Milton Keynes: color coding shows how residential (cream) and employment (mauve) areas are interspersed, with "green corridors" between them.

Working at Home

New technology makes it possible for people to work at home instead of commuting to a central workplace. They can link up via telephones and computers, including portable "lap-top" computers, and send plans or reports by fax through the telephone network. This is called "tele-commuting." Working at home has the advantages that you don't have to dress in a business suit; you can live where you want to; and you don't waste time or money traveling to work. So long as you complete your work on time, you can do it to fit in with your family or personal life.

This telecommuter appears to have the best of both worlds. However, for the sake of her health, she should take regular breaks from working at the computer screen.

Thousands of miles may separate them, but they can still discuss business face to face.

Tele-conferences

Some business people now link up via satellite and television screens to hold international conferences. This saves time, energy, and the cost of traveling long distances by air to meet face to face. It also saves on hotel bills. As more business is conducted at an international level, meetings and conferences of this kind may become standard practice.

9

The Healthy Office

Pictured here is a new style, healthy open-plan office. Unlike many offices built from the 1960s onward, the room has a high ceiling so that air can circulate, and people do not feel hemmed in. Natural light comes from large windows, so they will avoid the headaches often caused by constant fluorescent lighting. Desks and chairs can be adjusted to suit the individual worker. Cables to the computers and telephones run below the floor, so there are no wires to trip over. Colors are soft, corners rounded, and the window glass is $1/2$ inch thick to keep out traffic noise.

Inside a new healthy office, in Westminster, London.

Factory of the Future

The Volvo car plant at Kalmar in Sweden has been designed to be a good working environment. The work areas are situated as much as possible along outer walls where windows provide daylight and a pleasant view. Noise levels are low. There is no "assembly line." Workers are grouped in teams: for example, one team assembles all the electrical parts of the car, another fits the interior. Each worker is able to do all the tasks for which the team is responsible and works up to 40 minutes on each car. From above, the factory is star-shaped. Each team has its own working area, its own entrance, changing room, and "coffee corner." In other words, the factory is divided into a number of small workshops. Working in this way is far less stressful and more satisfying for everyone.

The car bodies are transported on battery-driven carriers controlled by cables in the floor. They are lifted and rotated so that the worker can stand comfortably.

Employers Are Responsible

In December 1991 two former keyboard operators were each awarded $10,500 damages in the first court case in Britain concerning repetitive strain injury. R.S.I. causes disabling pain, especially in the hands and wrists, and occurs where people perform repetitive physical tasks for lengthy periods. In this case, the workers used to complete 10,000 key-strokes an hour at computer terminals. The court found that the employers, British Telecom, were at fault. Now the problem has been clearly identified, and responsibility placed on employers to provide correctly designed seats and desks, and to allow sufficient breaks from repetitive tasks.

Home Comforts in a Tough Environment

Workers on large-scale construction or engineering projects far from home - for example, those building dams or roadways - have traditionally been expected to "rough it," living in makeshift huts or trailers. But advances in technology have created work in even more remote and dangerous places - for instance, on off-shore oil rigs. Such work requires

Smoke-Free

In the United States concern about the bad effects of cigarette smoking on the health of both smokers and non-smokers has led to common acceptance that workplaces should be smoke-free. Some workers have sued their employers for ill-health caused by other people smoking. Companies wishing to phase out smoking allow smokers a fixed time in which to give up, and some offer classes or **counseling**, but as a last resort workers who go on smoking may be fired.

On the best rigs, meals are described as being of high-class hotel standard.

highly skilled and physically fit engineers, geophysicists, and others. To recruit them, the drilling companies have to provide the best possible living and working conditions. The larger rigs in the North Sea accommodate as many as 150 workers, working 12-hour **shifts**. When not working they can watch television or work out in the fitness room. Sleeping accommodation is in single or shared cabins. Typically the men work two weeks on the rig, then have two weeks home leave before returning.

11

PROBLEMS AND PREJUDICES

As well as the physical hazards of work, many people face problems of a different kind. Hours of work often make it difficult to maintain personal and family life. Some people find it hard to get a job because they have a physical or mental disability, and even when in work they may suffer unfair **discrimination**. Members of minority communities and of particular racial groups often experience discrimination, too. And working women the world over find they are expected to compete against men for work or promotion on unfair terms. As a result, even today the majority are confined to low-paid and **low-status** jobs.

Action on Insulting Behavior

Since women workers have begun to speak out about sexual harassment (being teased or pestered in a way which they find embarrassing or distressful), some employers have adopted firm policies. British Rail, the publicly-owned railroad company, issues all its staff with a leaflet stating that such conduct will not be tolerated, and warning that offenders can be disciplined and dismissed. The company also provides counselors to give confidential advice and support to women who have suffered this demeaning and sometimes frightening experience.

Support for the Disabled

People with disabilities have proved that with common-sense provision, such as ramps for wheelchair access, they can do many jobs as well as anyone else. The Americans with Disabilities Act protects against discrimination and requires equal opportunity employment for the disabled. All companies employing 15 or more workers must extend equal opportunity and nondiscriminatory treatment to disabled employees and jobseekers. The British Civil Service has a policy covering recruitment, career development, accommodation, and equipment, and the safety of its disabled employees. Trade unions are increasingly aware of the needs of disabled workers, and are active in negotiating on their behalf.

Having a disability need not be a barrier to having a job and doing it well.

A Fairer System At Last

The wealth of South Africa is based on its gold and diamond mines, yet for years under the apartheid system black miners experienced some of the worst working and living conditions imaginable. Confined to work camps hundreds of miles away from their families, and able to return home only once every two years, thousands have suffered injury and death because of inadequate safety provision. Until 1983 it was illegal for them even to hold meetings or organize a trade union. Now, after a long struggle and with support from campaigners around the world, they look forward to political change that will bring them safer and fairer conditions of work as well as human rights.

Black miners in South Africa look forward to a better future.

Removing Discrimination

In the United States, Britain, and other countries, women and members of minority communities have won the legal right to be treated fairly at work. If unsuccessful in arguing their case with employers, they are able to seek a judgement from an **industrial tribunal**. Some attend assertiveness courses, to learn how to put forward their point of view in an effective way. Most employers now recognize that certain groups suffer unfair treatment, and many have adopted detailed positive action or **equal opportunities** policies, covering issues such as equal pay, equal opportunities for training and promotion, how jobs are advertised, and how appointments are made.

Thanks to laws against discrimination as well as a change of attitudes, this woman and thousands like her can do work previously reserved for men.

LEARNING THROUGHOUT YOUR LIFE

In Japan, 98 percent of pupils stay in school until they are eighteen. Students at this crammer school in Tokyo are under intense pressure to pass their exams.

In modern societies the pace of change is fast. The number of **unskilled** jobs has been shrinking, and employers need more well-trained workers with skills that can be adapted as the need arises. It used to be that the majority of children left school at fourteen or fifteen, and only the minority stayed on to gain qualifications. Today, all children in the United States must attend school up to the age of sixteen; and most receive further education or training through school, college, or trade schools; or through an **apprenticeship**, training program or **day release**. In some countries this trend toward extended periods of education is more marked.

However, there is a price. Many Japanese children suffer stress because of the pressure on them to pass exams; some even commit suicide. In many countries young people do not earn a decent salary until well into their twenties, which means they tend to delay getting married and having children. Students all around the world have to struggle to make ends meet. Some governments encourage them to borrow money to complete their studies, but this discourages children from poorer families. It also leaves them with a burden of debt once they do start to earn.

Technology changes so fast that skills need frequent updating. As patterns of employment change, many adults find themselves beginning new careers – sometimes more than once – and this means yet more training.

Making Links

Schools are increasingly encouraged to make links with employers in their local communities. Some school students have the chance to visit places of work as part of the curriculum, in order to talk to managers and workers and find out what a particular job is really like. Some regularly attend a workplace such as a store, or factory, or office, as part of work experience programs.

Many schools offer a work-study program, as well as provide courses in basic and advanced business skills.

Work experience in a hospital will help these students choose a career.

Pupils at Bwiru School carry water and cement to build a local corn mill. In return for their work their school receives a grant.

Necessary Skills

Tanzania, like other developing countries, badly needs the energies and skills of its most able young people. At secondary schools, the emphasis is on education for self-reliance. As well as an academic education, the pupils are instilled with a respect for physical work, and the needs of the local community. Government-funded schools are expected to raise part of their own income. Bwiru Girls' School has a farm where students work to grow cotton, corn, and tomatoes – all this on top of their normal school day.

Local Initiative for the Jobless

Leader of the Tower Hill Project, Steve Dumbell was unemployed for eight years. Now he aims to turn this derelict barn into a skills center for young people without jobs.

On the Tower Hill housing estate in Kirkby, Liverpool, in the early 1990s one in three people – including eight out of ten school dropouts – were unemployed. Being out of work leaves young people frustrated and angry; some may drift into vandalism and crime, further damaging the local community. Rather than go on waiting for help or investment from outside, local residents decided to try their own remedy. Campaigners set up the Tower Hill Community Trust to offer education and training, and give support to those wanting to set up small businesses. A council office, fitted out, provides workshops for services and light industry.

The Right To Training

In the United States, many companies offer tuition reimbursement to employees attending work-related courses, schooling, or training. Many European countries give workers a legal right to **study leave**, sometimes with pay. In France, all workers are entitled to paid **vocational training**. In Denmark public sector workers are allowed 1-2 years' study leave, depending on how long they have worked. In Spain workers have a legal right to paid exam leave, and in the engineering industry they can have 12 months' leave "for human and professional development." People increasingly welcome the chance to undertake training. It not only helps them find better jobs and higher rates of pay; it also gives them confidence, personal satisfaction, and skills they can use in other areas of their lives.

Working Under the Sun

A V.S.O. worker trains vehicle mechanics in Bafata, Guinea-Bissau.

In countries under colonial rule, schools and books were based on those in the imperial country. They were inappropriate to the children's real needs. Even after independence, students in these countries were often equipped for a western way of work, which meant they left their villages to seek prosperity either in the city or in a more developed country. Governments in both rich and poor countries now recognize the problems this causes. One response from the European Community is to help fund programs of practical training in developing countries. Organizations like Voluntary Service Overseas (V.S.O.) or Skillshare also help.

In Kenya, the Youth Training Support Program aims to improve training in metalwork, carpentry, masonry, and tailoring. The idea is that young workers then start their own businesses, bringing work to the districts where they live instead of flocking to the cities. It is hoped they will join a part of the local workforce known as the *Jua Kali*, which means "working under the sun."

Adult workers return to the classroom to update their technical skills at Tegel Airport, Berlin.

16

Training Valued

At the Japanese-owned Nissan car plant in Sunderland, in the north of England, staff received an average of 23.7 days of training in one year. The amount spent on training, $11.4 million, was equal to 14.5 per cent of the total wages bill. Other employers spend far less, but they may need to give workers similar opportunities if they are not to lose them. It is common for employers to try to "poach" skilled workers from each other. Some companies are now considering asking for a "transfer fee" when trained workers move on.

Open Learning

Courses open to the general public and correspondence courses (where teachers communicate with students by mail, by telephone, or via the broadcast media) are valuable to adults who cannot easily uproot themselves or their families to attend full-time classes. In Britain, the Open University has enabled over 100,000 people to graduate during the first twenty years of its existence. Students study at home in their spare time, and no previous qualifications are needed to join. Many women have gained degrees while at home raising their children; some people have qualified while serving a prison sentence, or while on a long-term hospital stay.

Access

Lack of confidence often holds people back from beginning a new career or restarting an old one. Many colleges now run courses for these people. Some are just for women, taught entirely by women. In this way people develop confidence, update their skills, and learn about the changed working environment. There are also "access" courses - introductory courses to prepare them for further education or training.

Women in Haringey, London, prepare for new careers with the help of a local Women's Training Center.

17

TIMES ARE CHANGING

A person's working life used to last from about age 16 to 65. People worked an 8-hour day, and a 5-day week, with extra hours as overtime, and they had a two-week vacation each year. Today, these fixed patterns are changing. Young people making their way and establishing a home work long hours, accepting high pressure. When they have children they demand more flexibility, with time off, part-time work, or hours to fit in with the school day. In Europe most workers are given four or six weeks' vacation each year, though American workers get far less.

Patterns of retirement are changing, too. For most people retirement still means having to live on a reduced or "fixed" income, and many feel a real sense of isolation or loss of purpose. However, better **pensions** and general prosperity give some the choice of retiring early and enjoying their leisure. Others prefer to go on working, perhaps part-time.

As more women work outside the home, supermarkets and banks have extended their opening hours so that working people can use them at convenient times. Longer opening hours have led to a need for more part-time workers for different shifts. Part-time work allows more women to work outside the home, but it is often poorly paid. The European Community aims to bring part-timers more into line with full-time workers.

A Shorter Working Week

In Japan, famous for hard work and industrial growth, opinion polls show that most people have begun to question the traditional long hours and short vacations. Instead of more work and more money they want an improvement in their quality of life. In 1990, the average Japanese manufacturing worker put in 2,080 hours, and many, including managers, worked much longer. Death from overwork - known as "karoshi" - is now officially recognized. In the early 1990s the government decided to reduce standard working hours to 1,800 a year (equivalent to 36 hours a week with 2 weeks' vacation). If successful, this will be an important first step in changing national attitudes and priorities.

Flexi-time

"Flexi-time" involves a core time, usually from 10 a.m. to 4 p.m., when employees must be present; a set period during which they may work, for instance, between 8 a.m. and 6 p.m.; and a set total of weekly or monthly hours they must complete. So long as they work during the core time and do sufficient hours in total, they can arrange the beginning and the end of the day to suit themselves. Many office workers in city banks and other businesses now work on this basis. Flexi-time has an extra value – it helps ease rush-hour traffic.

Those who are fortunate find work in which they can express themselves throughout life.

Helping the children cross safely: this elderly man enjoys staying active and earns a small wage to boost his pension.

Job Sharing: Advantages All Around

In a job-share one full-time post is divided between two people. They may each work half days, 2$^1/_2$ days a week, alternate weeks, or even in six-month blocks. Each worker gets half pay and half **benefits**, including sick leave, and vacations. Job-shares are popular with women professionals. For example, Sue Osborne and Susan Williams share a post as chief executive in the health service in South London. Their employers gain the advantage of two people's talent and training. The women are able to do satisfying, highly paid work, while still having part of the week to devote to themselves and their families.

Staying Active

On average, people live longer than they used to. In Europe, by the year 2040, one person in five will be retired, with even higher proportions in Switzerland and Germany, and it is expected that they will be increasingly fit and active. More than ever they run small businesses, or become **consultants**, or do routine or careperson work, letting younger people bear the strain of high-pressure decision-making jobs. Laws about retirement, taxation and pensions are having to be rewritten to take account of this new extension to people's working lives.

AN OLD-FASHIONED STRUCTURE

Traditional work organizations are like a pyramid. Most workers are on the bottom and the bigger the organization, the more layers of management there are. Those at the top are paid the most and only they can make key decisions. Working in such organizations can be unpleasant. Things often get tied up in red tape: middle managers are afraid to make decisions and those at the bottom often feel alienated and undervalued.

A private company's overall purpose is to make profits for owners and **investors**. These may be prominent individuals, other companies, or anonymous **shareholders**. Unlike employees, they are not tied to one firm, but can invest in lots of different enterprises in the hope of profits and **dividends**. Many workers not only never meet the boss - they also have no idea who owns their company! Sometimes a conflict of interest can arise, for example when directors decide to move a company to another country where workers accept lower wages.

In both the capitalist world and the former communist countries many people are trying to get rid of the pyramid and introduce fair rewards and more democracy at work.

Employees at the Mitsubishi Motor Corporation in Okazaki, Japan, work in small teams, or *"quality circles." They plan the work together and share responsibility for its proper completion.*

Community and Cooperation

In the United States there are now 10,000 firms with employee stock ownership - where workers own at least a part of the company they work for and share in any profits. America also has 1,000 small business **cooperatives** or **collectives**, and more than 1,000 other enterprises run on democratic lines. They include bakeries, food coops, bookstores, health centers, house renovators, farms, taxi firms, and solar panel makers. Their workers have voting rights and participate directly in decision making.

Teamwork

The Volvo car assembly plant opened in Uddevalla, southwest Sweden, in 1988, is hailed as a further advance on the revolutionary Kalmar factory (see page 10). Company president Roger Holtback says they are going back to the "old, well-proven system of apprentices and **master craftsmen**... who felt professional pride and dignity and identified deeply with their work." The new factory uses ultra-modern engineering and computer technology, but the assembly area has no robots. Teamwork is the key to friendship and co-operation between workers - 40 per cent of whom are women. Each team directs its own work, and in this plant assembles the whole car. There are no supervisors or foremen. It is interesting that workers at Kalmar and Uddevalla take sick days less than half as often as those in other plants.

At Uddevalla small teams work without a foreman or supervisor.

The Big Carrot

The Big Carrot is a worker-owned organic food store in Toronto, Canada. In just six years during the 1980s it grew from a small collective employing 9 people to a supermarket employing 69. Like many new co-operative enterprises, the Big Carrot has developed from the ideas of the Green movement. It tries to uphold Green principles both in terms of the products it sells and by being a humane employer. As part of this philosophy, it has given financial support to other worker cooperatives and to organic farmers.

Networking

Certain large companies now rely on having a smaller "core" of full-time workers, and "buying in" work from independent outsiders such as designers, accountants, or editors. Many of these professionals enjoy the independence of working from home, but they can feel isolated. One way to overcome this problem is through "networking" - hooking up with other people for particular projects. Some home workers organize local work clubs, where they share meeting rooms and equipment.

The Big Carrot food store. They work in it; they own it; they enjoy its success.

THE IMPACT OF TECHNOLOGY

We already have the self-cleaning public toilet, designed so that the toilet bowl and the floor are automatically washed and disinfected after every use. Robots assemble cars, and refill warehouse shelves. We have driverless trains. Thanks to biotechnology we should soon have the self-cleaning ship, coated with a biological substance to repel barnacles. One day we may have voice-sensitive computers, able to translate the spoken word into writing on a screen, so that even typing will not be necessary.

New technology solves some problems but creates others. In developed countries many jobs have disappeared, particularly manual jobs, and although there are new industries, these do not provide enough jobs for everyone. In developing countries, with growing populations, the problem is more acute. If governments borrow money to buy high-tech machinery, they not only sink further into debt but also push more people out of work. The main challenge for them is to introduce appropriate and affordable tools and machines, creating work in villages and towns where people need it.

"Small Is Beautiful"

Many people have turned away from large-scale industrial development toward a greater concern for the environment. They regret the way modern cities and products all look alike. The result has been a revival of traditional crafts in developed countries, and a strong movement to maintain them in poorer parts of the world. Many people find great personal satisfaction in making things by hand, whether for sale or for their own use. Once, crafts such as knitting or cabinet making were handed down in families, but industrialization disrupts this process, and such skills can die out. In the United States, craftwork has found new life in the past decade, with a wealth of courses and seminars, and craft shows and festivals held throughout the country. Handcrafted items are much valued for their quality and skill in creation.

Reviving a skilled craft - and conserving a beautiful village.

Bicycle trailer made in a local workshop in South India, with support from the Intermediate Technology group.

Appropriate Technology

In developing countries it is important for new technology to ENHANCE local work, not wipe it out. In India and Sri Lanka development workers helped design a bicycle trailer strong enough to take heavy loads, yet able to be made in local workshops. One young man who carried the local fisherwomen's catch to market five miles away found that he could carry much bigger loads than when using just his bicycle, and this meant he had higher earnings. He even adapted the trailer to include seats, so that he could carry four people as well. With its strong, low-cost wheels the trailer will also be of great benefit to farmers and others to transport their goods.

In Matara district, south Sri Lanka, blacksmiths have been trying out a new, locally-made power hammer. It will enable them to double their work producing and repairing tools. The old hand-held hammer was very heavy, but thanks to the power hammer, for the first time a woman has been able to start work as a smith.

Green Jobs

The ecology movement worldwide has had an impact on the types of work many people do. Organic farming needs more workers than intensive farming, because controlling weeds and fertilizing the soil without the use of chemicals involves hoeing and digging and keeping a close watch on crops. Recycling is a growing industry that hardly existed in most countries before the 1980s. Conservation and countryside management provide new socially useful careers. In Germany there are an estimated 14,000 enterprises based on green ideas and alternative life-styles, employing 30,000 people. They run their own network of support, finance, and publications.

Susy Dunkerton, organic farmer and proud of it, prepares apples to make cider.

UNPAID AND INVISIBLE

In poor countries children have to work hard to help provide for their families' basic needs. When parents become ill or die, older children shoulder the burden of caring for younger brothers and sisters.

Some of the most important work done in any society takes place in the home. It includes cooking, washing clothes, cleaning, and paying bills on time. In poorer countries it may involve walking several miles each day to fetch water or gather firewood. It also includes caring for children: catering to their physical needs, giving them love and support, teaching them to talk, and helping them develop the personal and social skills they need to survive. Another important job is to care for those who are ill or infirm.

Traditionally this "housework" has been done almost exclusively by women inside families. It has always been undervalued. It is unpaid. It never figures in government statistics of the **Gross National Product**. If a man hires a housekeeper and pays her wages, she is considered part of the workforce. But if the man marries her, and she goes on doing the same work for no wages, she somehow becomes "invisible!"

Housework Made Visible

In recent years housework has been given at least some recognition. Divorce court judges accept that a wife's unpaid work contributes to the home, and should entitle her to a fair share if property is to be divided up. The Legal and General Insurance company estimated in 1988 that if housework was paid work, it would be worth about $665 per week. In the United States, child support and maintenance are paid directly to divorced mothers. Women see this benefit as at least some recognition of the work they do.

Many fathers are much more involved in child care than men in earlier generations and enjoy the closeness this brings.

Caring and Sharing

In some cultures the roles of men and women are quite separate and differences strictly enforced. But in the United States, Europe and elsewhere, most people have come to believe in more equal forms of partnership, helped by measures such as equal opportunities and **maternity** and **paternity leave**. Occasionally, couples reverse the traditional pattern so that the man stays at home while the woman goes out to work. Young people sharing a house, perhaps while at college, often devise a schedule to share the housework fairly. Nevertheless, surveys all around the world show that even when women go out to work, they still do most of the work at home as well, especially washing and ironing, making the evening meal, taking care of sick children, and general cleaning.

Having a Choice

Early this century, people of quite modest means would have a servant or housekeeper to clean the house and care for the children. Later, inventions such as the vacuum cleaner and the washing machine enabled housework to be done without servants.

When women began to work outside the home in greater numbers, there were new changes. Some things previously made by women in the home - from cakes to clothes - were produced commercially instead. Also some of the careperson work, which women had done unpaid at home, became paid work - from taking care of children during the day to caring for patients in hospital.

In recent years there has been a return to the employment of nannies or domestic help, and a huge increase in types of domestic appliance and convenience food. But some people have chosen a different life-style, sometimes earning less in order to spend more time at home, whether to bake their own bread or be with their children. These patterns affect the lives of individual adults and children, and ultimately society and the environment. Most people would not claim to have all the answers, but if they are lucky they can have freedom of choice.

A mother takes her baby to a preschool day-care nursery. Today parents of young children tend to live far away from their own parents, brothers and sisters, on whom they might once have called for help. Women's support groups, baby-sitting circles, and preschool play groups help fill the gap.

25

WHO CARES?

Many countries provide a range of welfare services employing nurses, doctors, social workers, and many more. Many charities have grown big enough to employ full-time professional staff. Some people thought these developments would bring an end to voluntary activity in the community, but they were wrong. Around the world there are organizations such as churches, trade unions, advice groups, and youth clubs where people work unpaid. Increasingly they act in partnership with official agencies; sometimes they fill gaps left by public services; but sometimes, as in the case of Amnesty International, they mobilize the concern of ordinary citizens against oppressive governments.

Self-help

Charity used to be thought of as people in more fortunate circumstances helping those less well-off, but a newer trend is toward self-help. People suffering from a particular illness, or who have been victims of crime or injustice, often discover skills and determination they never knew they had. One self-help group was set up in London in the early 1980s by a couple of mothers whose babies cried all the time. They were at their wits' ends until they got together to give mutual support. Now CRY-SIS is a nationwide organization.

A New Lifeline

With a telephone in just about every home, volunteers are able to provide around-the-clock counseling, and have the satisfaction of helping strangers on a one-to-one basis. For example, the Samaritans, named after the good Samaritan in the Bible story, are always available to help unhappy people pull back from the brink of committing suicide. The Youth Crisis and Runaway Hotline is a 24-hour, toll-free help line. Volunteers provide a sympathetic, anonymous listening service for children who may have no one else to talk to about their problems.

Experiencing a problem yourself helps you understand what others are going through and how to help them. Self-help group CRY-SIS was built on this principle.

A Fast Response When the Need is Great

In 1990, two teachers and a welfare assistant at a school in Britain were horrified by television pictures of children abandoned in orphanages in Romania. The women - Helen Turner, Islay MacArdle, and Annette Virgette - decided to help. They raised money, collected equipment and toys from friends and neighbors, then drove a 7½-ton truck 3,500 miles across Europe to deliver them. On their

Loading equipment for orphanages in Romania: volunteers who went to help said it changed their lives.

return, they wrote a report about what else could be done. In times of emergency, ordinary people are often the first to respond - even from the other side of the world. Frequently they may shame governments into doing more.

The Appeal of Television

Television has remarkable power to galvanize people into action for the community. An example is *Anneka's Challenge*, a B.B.C. television program. Viewers write to Anneka Rice, the presenter, with a challenge, which she opens in front of the cameras. The challenge must be completed within a set time, usually just two or three days. Anneka sets about telephoning and visiting people, persuading them to help. Often a huge army of volunteers is organized, many offering specialized skills and

People of all ages respond to Anneka's Challenge.

equipment, and the cameras record their work. A new pier has been built on an off-shore island; a home for stray dogs reconstructed; a derelict lighthouse renovated. People gladly participate knowing that the end-result is worthwhile, and that their efforts will be recognized when the program is broadcast. On a smaller scale, local radio and television, through charity appeals and phone-ins, serve as the contact between volunteers and work that needs doing.

Self-help to Learning in the Third Age

The French coined a term, *Le Troisième Age*, to refer to people who have come through their first age - learning, and their second age - working. The Third Age is seen as the age of living. In France and in Britain, people exchange skills and knowledge, teaching or learning subjects which interest them, at meetings of an organization called the University of the Third Age. Voluntary organizations rely increasingly on the active elderly. They have taken over from younger married women who now go out to work.

For decades, billions of dollars and the most advanced technology went into making weapons. Since the end of the "cold war" in Europe, the arms industry has been cut back.

Workers in the former Soviet Union are here dismantling weapons. What will they make next?

No one can be sure where all this change will lead, but some patterns do point strongly to the future.

We can expect governments to play an increasing role in improving working life. The United States and most countries within the European Community already fix a minimum wage level to help low earners; set standards of safety to protect people at work; and give employees specific legal rights against unfair treatment. As countries continue to draw together through international agreements, these measures will tend to become harmonized. However, it is not clear how many of them will take the necessary steps to tackle the problem of unemployment.

Those who work in organizations, whether publicly or privately owned, will come to have more say in how their work is organized. As ideas about democracy and freedom of information grow in the rest of society, people will expect them to apply in the workplace. More employees will receive training and be highly skilled. They will work more and more on their own initiative, dealing with new problems and untried situations. Many will have flexible working arrangements to fit in with family and personal life. Some will choose work - paid and unpaid - that is personally fulfilling and accords with their concern for the environment. They will draw up "environmental audits" to ensure that their workplace does not add to the problems of pollution or waste.

More efforts will have to be made at an international level to help provide work and security in developing countries. This will involve economic measures to help them with their burden of debt. Without such measures, the young people of these countries will continue to migrate to places where they can find greater prosperity.

These are the author's predictions. But part of the future belongs to you. By your choices you, too, can affect the changing patterns of work.

GLOSSARY

apprenticeship An agreement whereby a young worker serves an employer for a certain number of years, in return for on-the-job training in a particular trade or craft, for example, dress making, or plumbing.

benefits Advantages or allowances sometimes given to workers in addition to their basic pay. These may include health insurance, an expense account, the right to parental leave, etc.

collective Organization or business run by a group of individuals for the benefit of all of them.

consultant Expert who advises or reports on aspects of work or business.

counseling Process where skilled listeners help individuals think through problems or decisions, sometimes giving advice.

day-release Program of training in which employees are released from work on regular days to attend courses run by local colleges or trade unions.

discrimination Any form of unfair distinction made between particular groups or individuals affecting their dignity, or rights and opportunities.

dividends Payments made to shareholders from a company's profits.

equal opportunities Policies or guidelines designed to counteract various forms of discrimination.

Gross National Product Total of everything a country has produced in a given year, including manufactured goods and services, as calculated by economists.

industrial tribunal Special court given the task of ruling on issues affecting employment and settling disputes between workers and employers.

investor Someone who buys shares, or who lends money to help a company develop or expand.

low-status Job or position generally thought of as less important than others, and often low-paid.

mass production Name given to large-scale factory process, in which identical products are made in large numbers.

master craftsman Skilled worker, for example, carpenter, stonemason, usually in business for his or her self.

Maternity/paternity leave Time off allowed to mothers and fathers at the time of the birth of a child, with or without pay.

pension Regular sum of money paid to a person of retirement age. State pensions (such as social security) come from programs of national insurance or taxation; other pensions come from separate pension funds to which workers and employers make regular payments. In effect, a pension is part of your earnings saved up for you to use in later life.

production line System of organization in a factory where identical products are passed between workers who stand or sit at fixed stations. Each worker repeats a separate task or set of tasks as the product passes from stage to stage.

profits The surplus money made by a company after all other moneys for raw materials, energy, salaries, etc. have been paid.

public sector Areas of work financed by government, such as health and welfare services.

shareholder Someone who holds a share in a company; shares are held in the form of certificates which can be bought and sold; their price goes up or down according to whether the company is thought to be successful.

shift Period of continuous working between set hours; term used especially in workplaces such as hospitals or factories where work goes on around the clock, for example, the night shift, the day shift.

study leave Block of time allowed away from work for education or training, paid or unpaid.

trade union Organization of employees in particular trades or industries, formed to represent their interests in various ways: for example, by bargaining with employers over pay and conditions; assisting members in difficulty and representing them at industrial tribunals; organizing training and social activities.

unskilled job Work, especially manual work, that does not require special training or qualifications.

vocational training Training designed to equip people for particular vocations or types of work.

workers' cooperative Organization owned and run by its own workers; several thousand of these exist in Spain, Italy and France.

Picture Credits:

J. Barrett 15T; Big Carrot 21B; Environmental Picture Library 3, 8, 23B; B. Prince/Format 12, 13B, 17: Four Millbank 10T; The Guardian 15B; Robert Harding Picture Library 20, 22; Sassoon/Robert Harding Picture Library 24; Schiller/Robert Harding Picture Library 9BL; Schuster/Robert Harding Picture Library 5L, 16R; Hutchison Library 26; M. Macintyre/Hutchison Library 14T; H. Sykes/Impact 11; Intermediate Technology 23T; S. & R. Greenhill 18; The Creative Company/Milton Keynes Development Corporation 9T; Lewis/Network 7; Pulitz/Network 19R; Sykes/Network 14B; C. Johnson/Panos 5R; Rex Features 27T; Roy Export Company Establishment 4; Run Riot Ltd. 27B; South-African Embassy 13T; Novosti/Frank Spooner Pictures 28; A. Fraser/VSO 16L; Volvo 10B, 21T; John Walmsley 9BR, 19L.

Cover photo: ZEFA

Helpful Organizations

EQUAL EMPLOYMENT ADVISORY COUNCIL
1015 15th Street NW, Suite 1220, Washington, D.C. 20005.
Tel: 202-789-8650
Distributes publications; conducts workshops; answers inquiries.

EQUAL EMPLOYMENT OPPORTUNITY COMMISSION LIBRARY
2401 E. Street NW, Room 242, Washington, D.C. 20507.
Tel: 202-634-6990.
Investigates charges of employment discrimination; answers inquiries; provides advisory assistance.

OFFICE OF INFORMATION AND CONSUMER AFFAIRS
Employment Standards Administration, Department of Labor, 3rd Street & Constitution Avenue NW, Washington, D.C. 20210.
Tel: 202-523-8743
Oversees administration of the Fair Labor Standards Act; answers inquiries; offers pamphlets; makes referrals.

Further Reading

Most books about patterns of work are aimed at adults. The following might be of interest, with the first two geared toward the young adult:

Doggell, Clinton L. *Equal Employment Opportunities Commission*. New York; Chelsea House, 1989.

Wainwright, Eric. *Trade Unions*. England; Batsford, 1984.

Flamholtz, Eric G. and Felicitas Hinman. *Future Directions of Employee Relations*. Los Angeles, CA; University of California Institute of Industrial Relations, 1986.

Robertson, James. *Future Work: Jobs, Self-Employment and Leisure After the Industrial Age*. New York; Universe Books, 1985.

INDEX

PRINTED IN BELGIUM BY
proost
INTERNATIONAL BOOK PRODUCTION